THEMATIC UNIT
BUBBLES

Written by Kimberly Robinson

Illustrated by Paula Spence

Teacher Created Materials, Inc.
P.O. Box 1040
Huntington Beach, CA 92647
©1991 Teacher Created Materials, Inc.
Made in U.S.A.

ISBN 1-55734-275-X

Table of Contents

Introduction

Bubbles contains a captivating whole language, thematic unit. Its 80 exciting pages are filled with a wide variety of lesson ideas and reproducible pages designed for use with primary children. At its core are two high-quality children's literature selections, *Never Snap at a Bubble* and *Professor Bubbles' Official Bubble Handbook*. For each of these books activities are included which set the stage for reading, encourage the enjoyment of the book, and extend the concepts gained. In addition, the theme is connected to the curriculum with activities in language arts (including daily writing suggestions), math, science, social studies, art, music, and life skills (cooking, physical education, career awareness, etc.) Many of these activities encourage cooperative learning. Suggestions and patterns for bulletin boards and unit management tools are additional time savers for the busy teacher. Furthermore, directions for student-created Big Books and a culminating activity, which allow students to synthesize their knowledge in order to produce products that can be shared beyond the classroom, highlight this very complete teacher resource.

This thematic unit includes:

- ❑ **literature selections**—summaries of two children's books with related lessons (complete with reproducible pages) that cross the curriculum

- ❑ **poetry**—suggested selections and lessons enabling students to write and publish their own works

- ❑ **planning guides**—suggestions for sequencing lessons each day of the unit

- ❑ **writing ideas**—daily suggestions as well as writing activities across the curriculum, including Big Wall Books and Window Books

- ❑ **bulletin board ideas**—suggestions and plans for student-created and/or interactive bulletin boards

- ❑ **homework suggestions**—extending the unit to the child's home

- ❑ **curriculum connections**—in language arts, math, science, social studies, art, music, and life skills such as cooking, physical education, and career awareness

- ❑ **group projects**—to foster cooperative learning

- ❑ **a culminating activity**—which requires students to synthesize their learning to produce a product or engage in an activity that can be shared with others

- ❑ **a bibliography**—suggesting additional literature and non-fiction books on the theme

---

To keep this valuable resource intact so that it can be used year after year, you may wish to punch holes in the pages and store them in a three-ring binder.

Introduction (cont.)

Why Whole Language?

A whole language approach involves children in using all modes of communication: reading, writing, listening, observing, illustrating, experiencing, and doing. Communication skills are interconnected and integrated into lessons that emphasize the whole of language rather than isolating its parts. The lessons revolve around selected literature. Reading is not taught as a separate subject from writing and spelling, for example. A child reads, writes (spelling appropriately for his/her level), speaks, listens, etc. in response to a literature experience introduced by the teacher. In this way, language skills grow naturally, stimulated by involvement and interest in the topic at hand.

Why Thematic Planning?

One very useful tool for implementing an integrated whole language program is thematic planning. By choosing a theme with correlating literature selections for a unit of study, a teacher can plan activities throughout the day that lead to a cohesive, in-depth study of the topic. Students will be practicing and applying their skills in meaningful contexts. Consequently, they will tend to learn and retain more. Both teachers and students will be freed from a day that is broken into unrelated segments of isolated drill and practice.

Why Cooperative Learning?

Besides academic skills and content, students need to learn social skills. No longer can this area of development be taken for granted. Students must learn to work cooperatively in groups in order to function well in modern society. Group activities should be a regular part of school life and teachers should consciously include social objectives as well as academic objectives in their planning. For example, a group working together to write a report may need to select a leader. The teacher should make clear to the students and monitor the qualities of good leader-follower group interaction just as he/she would state and monitor the academic goals of the project.

Why Big Books?

An excellent cooperative, whole language activity is the production of Big Books. Groups of students, or the whole class, can apply their language skills, content knowledge, and creativity to produce a Big Book that can become a part of the classroom library to be read and reread. These books make excellent culminating projects for sharing beyond the classroom with parents, librarians, other classes, etc. Big Books can be produced in many ways and this thematic unit book includes directions for at least one method you may choose.

Never Snap at a Bubble

by Yvonne Winer and Carol Aitken McLean-Carr

Summary

This story and its illustrations will spark the wonder of bubbles. Students will discover rhythm, repetition, and sentence structure as the themes of family, counting, bubble science, self-image, and responsibility are explored. This book is available in both Big and little book sizes.

Baby Frog is fascinated with the pond's bubbles. He ignores his parents repeated warnings, "Never snap at a bubble." As he swallows the bubbles, he stretches and stretches like a balloon. The creatures of the pond watch in amazement as Baby Frog faces the consequences of not listening.

The outline below is a suggested plan for using the various activities that are presented in this unit. You may adapt these ideas to fit your own classroom situations.

Sample Plan

Day I

- Introduce unit with bulletin board activity (page 71)
- Do "My Bubble Brainstorm": pre-reading strategy (page 10)
- Get acquainted with bubbles
- Complete Story Frame (page 13)
- Read *Never Snap at a Bubble* aloud to class; predict ending (page 6)
- Bubbleologist Journal (page 28)
- Assign homework: The Search for Bubbles (page 6)
- **Remind students to bring in small containers to store bubble solutions!**

Day II

- Book Talks (page 6)
- Bubble Trivia (page 27)
- Complete Bubble Journey Worksheet (page 14)
- Make Bubble Collage (page 66)
- Make Bubbleologist Bubble Solution (page 68)
- Bobbin' Bubble Poems (page 38)
- Science: News on Bubbles (page 58)
- Continue Bubbleologist Journal (page 28)
- Create Floating Frog (page 66)
- Design Bubble Bookmarks (page 11)

Day III

- Continue Bubble Trivia (page 27)
- Creative Writing: Bubble-toons (page 29)
- Math: The Longest Frog Race (page 53)
- Complete Story Sequence Strips (page 16)
- Bubble Lollipops (page 68)
- Continue Bubbleologist Journal (page 28)

Day IV

- Continue Bubble Trivia (page 27)
- Poem: Bubble Square Dance (page 42)
- Science/math: Bubble Patterns (page 61)
- Comprehension: Story Summary (page 17)
- Bubble Thoughts creative writing (page 33)
- Create bubble invitations (page 7)
- Wall Book (page 18)
- Design Bubble Jar Labels (page 40)

Day V

- Creative Writing: Bubbles Magically Escape (page 32)
- Bubble Window Book (page 18)
- The Deep Dive for Rhyming (page 46)
- Bubble Party Day (page 7)

Overview of Activities

SETTING THE STAGE

1. Create a bubbly mood by making the bulletin board display (pages 71 to 75). Follow directions on page 71 to use the bulletin board as a unit introduction.

2. Set up a learning center that challenges students to explore the world of bubbles (page 8). Display a variety of bubble paraphernalia (blowers, wands, straw frames, cans) and books (page 80) at the learning center. This will be a great start to help students get acquainted with bubbles.

3. Recite the delightful poem "Bubble Square Dance" (page 42). Students will move with excitement as they learn the words, body movements, and create bubble fairy stick puppets on page 65. Turn the poem into a captivating bubble play.

4. Brew Bubble Solution (recipe, page 68) for each student to use as they experience skills in measurement, predictions, and observations of bubbles.

5. Complete Bubble Pet science project on page 63.

ENJOYING THE BOOK

1. Show students the cover of *Never Snap at a Bubble*. Have them complete the "Before" section of page 13. Read the story, stopping before the last page. Have students illustrate their predicted endings. Finish reading the story; then discuss the predicted pictures and complete the story frame. Have students illustrate or write a sequel telling what happens to Baby Frog after using the story summary worksheet (page 17).

2. **Homework Activity:** Send students (parents can help) on a bubbly adventure as they search through old magazines, books, objects, or brainstorm a list of things, animals, or people making bubbles. Cut out the pictures, collect the items, or draw bubbly pictures or words. Then create a bubble collage described on page 66.

3. Read or have students read other bubble or frog stories (see Bibliography, page 80). Watch the fuse ignite in your students as they engage in "Book Talks."

    a. After reading or hearing a book, students complete Book Talk Note (page 12).

    b. Students drop them in a designated Book Talk can or box.

    c. At a set time each day, a student chooses a note from the Book Talk can. The chosen Book Talk notewriter presents his/her story.

Overview of Activities *(cont.)*

4. Reread *Never Snap at a Bubble* spending time with each illustration. Discuss each character's expressions, moods, and responses. Complete a character rating checklist as a class or in a small group (page 15). Pictures from the book can be used as story starters. Complete the story sequencing worksheet (page 16).

5. Complete a selection of the activities listed in the Sample Plan (page 5) and described on pages 27-70.

EXTENDING THE BOOK

1. Take a field trip to the nearest nursing home. What an exciting visit for the elderly! Have students demonstrate their homemade bubble wands, personally published bubble stories and poems, bubble songs, and the bubble square dance. Display students finished bubble art work on the Nursing Home's bulletin board.

2. For variation in reading group styles try buddies (partners take turns reading), choral reading, independent, or auditory awareness (listening to a story on tape).

3. Finale! Throw a party! Have students share their new-found knowledge of bubbles with another classroom.

   • Students write and design their own bubble invitations or use the ones on page 77.

   • Share bubble poetry on pages 44-45 created by the students.

   • Have a bubble gum blowing contest. Who can blow the biggest bubble or start a bubble the fastest?

   • Give bubble awards (e.g., for the best designed wand, story, or poem on bubbles). Note: Make sure **all** students receive an award.

   • Let your guests enjoy the bubbles Learning Center Activities.

   • Provide bubbly punch and refreshments.

   • As a departing gift, give samples of the bubbleologist bubble solution for guests to take home!

Creating a Learning Center

A learning center is a special area set aside in the classroom for the study of a specific topic. Typically, a learning center contains a variety of activities and materials that teach, reinforce, and enrich skills and concepts. Because students learn in different ways and at different rates, a learning center can be a valuable means of providing for these differences. Activities in a given center should be based on the abilities, needs, and interests of the students in your classroom. Learning Centers are equally appropriate for cooperative groups and individual use.

How To Create a Learning Center

- Select a topic or theme in any subject area (e.g. Bubbles).
- Label the center attractively with a display or poster.
- Determine specific skills or concepts to be taught or reinforced (parts of a bubble, bubble syllables or contractions).
- Develop appropriate learning activities (Bubble Gameboard, page 59, Bubble Bookmarks, page 11).
- Prepare extended activities for reinforcement or enrichment (Bubble Collage on page 66).
- Gather all materials needed to complete the projects at the center (paint, scissors, construction paper, glue.)

Scheduling Center Time

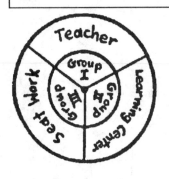

- Plan a schedule where students rotate to the different activities. For example, one group can be attending a teacher-directed lesson, while the second group completes seat work, and the third group is at the Learning Center.
- Assign individuals or small groups to the center activities according to the diagnosed needs.
- Have a set center time each day. Assign a different group each day to work at the center during that time.

Record Keeping

- You may supply each student with a learning center record keeper and a weekly calendar. Store in 3-ring binder at center.
- Keep a file box with students' names listed alphabetically on index cards. Record notes and activities completed on the cards.

8

Bubble Web

A web can be useful in the following ways:
- To determine prior knowledge of theme
- To help students organize their thoughts
- To serve as an evaluation tool

1. Before beginning a thematic unit, allow students to brainstorm and orally express all they know about the thematic unit concept. On large chart paper draw a circle in the center and place the thematic unit concept inside the circle. Draw lines from the circle and write the students' responses on the lines. **All** responses are to be written down. The responses will help you to determine what they really do know about the theme concept, and can be invaluable in determining your lesson plans. Use illustrations and words with younger children.

2. Creating a web allows students to focus their thoughts. As the thematic unit is being taught, students can evaluate their web in an ongoing manner, updating or changing facts stated on the web. Have students complete their individual bubble brainstorm (page 10). Store in bubble journal and as they learn something new, or desire to change a previously stated response, they simply make the changes on their own web.

3. As an evaluation tool refer to the original web used at the beginning of thematic unit. Reread the initial responses given. Using a different color marker, make deletions (crossing out incorrect responses) or add new knowledge on additional lines. Compare the initial responses to the deletions or additions to evaluate the students knowledge gained through the thematic unit presented.

9

Name _____   *Never Snap at a Bubble*

My Bubble Brainstorm

Directions: Complete questions below and store in your Bubbleologist Journal folder.

What do I know about bubbles?

_____

_____

_____

_____

What do I want to learn about bubbles?

_____

_____

_____

_____

_____

Check off as you learn!

_____

_____

_____

_____

_____

What I am learning about bubbles.

_____

_____

How To Make Bubble Bookmarks

These bookmarks can be an educational tool for your students. The lines provided on each bookmark can be used for students to jot down new reading words, spelling words, or words demonstrating a specific skill (contractions, plurals, nouns).

Directions

Copy the patterns and directions below. Mount directions on colored strips of construction paper. Have students complete this activity at the Learning Center site. Supply a variety of materials (tissue paper, glitter, cellophane paper, sequins, markers, scissors).

1. **Choose** one bookmark pattern.

2. **Color** and **design** bookmark.

3. **Glue** to a piece of construction paper...Let dry!

4. **Cut** on dotted lines.

Design your own

I'm bubbling into reading!

I go 'bubbles' over reading

Book Talks

Title: _____

Author: _____

Answer these questions:

 1. Why did you choose this book? _____

   _____

 2. Read your favorite sentence or word from the book.

 3. My favorite picture is on page _____

 4. What happens in the beginning of the story? _____

   _____

   _____

 5. SECRET! Don't share the ending...let your classmates guess until they have read the book.

Written By: _____

Title: _____

Author: _____

Answer these questions:

 1. Why did you choose this book? _____

   _____

 2. Read your favorite sentence or word from the book.

 3. My favorite picture is on page _____

 4. What happens in the beginning of the story? _____

   _____

   _____

 5. SECRET! Don't share the ending...let your classmates guess until they have read the book.

Written By: _____

Story Frame

Directions: Look at cover of book and make predictions about what might happen in the story.

1. Make your predictions (guesses) by answering questions in the **before** bubbles.

2. Listen to the story being read.

3. Then complete the **after** bubbles.

4. How close were your predictions?

Before I read the story:

Who is in the story?

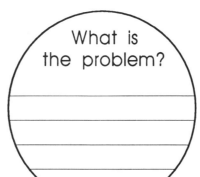

What is the problem?

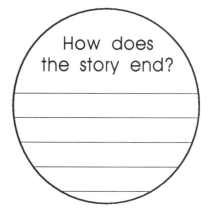

How does the story end?

- -

After I read the story:

Who is in the story?

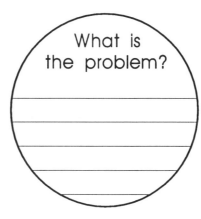

What is the problem?

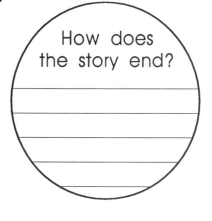

How does the story end?

The Bubble Journey

Directions: Fill in the blanks by using the word bank. First read through the story. It will make filling in the blanks easier!

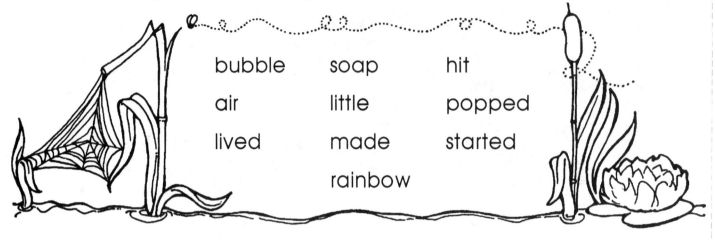

bubble	soap	hit
air	little	popped
lived	made	started
	rainbow	

Once there _____ a little _____. It was filled with _____. The air _____ the bubble float. It floated from cloud to cloud. The _____ bubble was covered with _____ and water. When sun rays _____ the soapy skin, it made beautiful _____ colors. The little bubble was getting tired. It _____ to turn black . . . .OH NO . . . the little bubble _____!

Use the story to complete the questions.

1. What is inside of a bubble? _____

2. What happens when a sun ray hits the bubble's soapy skin? ___

_____

3. What does it mean when a bubble turns black? _____

_____

4. On the back of this paper draw a picture of a bubble with your favorite person, place, or thing!

Character Rating

Directions: Color in the box that completes the character rating.

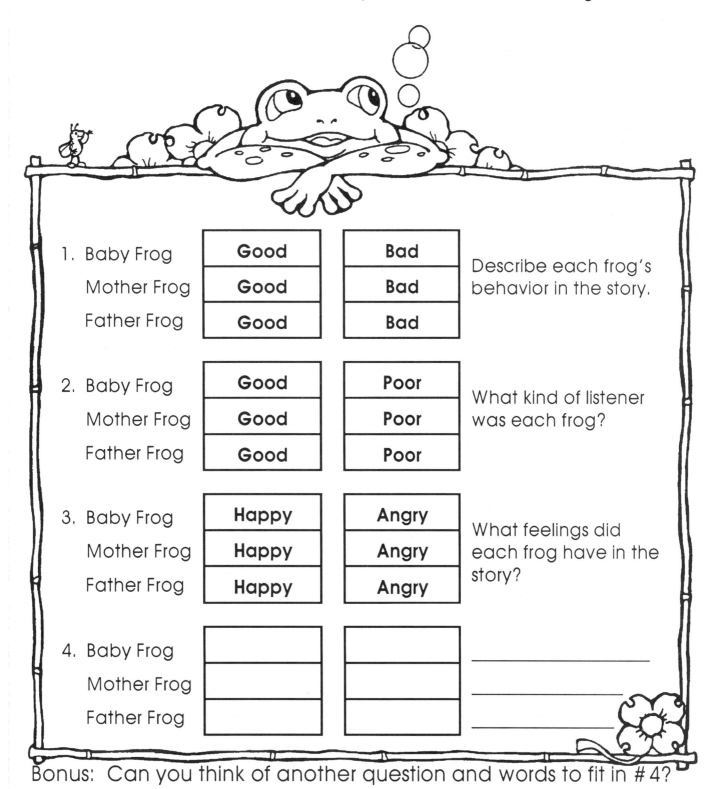

1. Baby Frog | **Good** | **Bad** | Describe each frog's
   Mother Frog | **Good** | **Bad** | behavior in the story.
   Father Frog | **Good** | **Bad** |

2. Baby Frog | **Good** | **Poor** | What kind of listener
   Mother Frog | **Good** | **Poor** | was each frog?
   Father Frog | **Good** | **Poor** |

3. Baby Frog | **Happy** | **Angry** | What feelings did
   Mother Frog | **Happy** | **Angry** | each frog have in the
   Father Frog | **Happy** | **Angry** | story?

4. Baby Frog | | | _____
   Mother Frog | | | _____
   Father Frog | | | _____

Bonus: Can you think of another question and words to fit in # 4?

15

Story Sequence Strips

Directions

1. **Work** with a partner.

2. **Cut** apart the sentence strips.

3. **Glue** each strip to a sheet of construction paper.

4. **Draw** a picture for each sentence.

5. Put the story pages **in order** so that it tells a story... then fasten one side to make a book! (Use staples or paper fasteners.)

6. **Enjoy** reading to your classmates!

And sailed away!
"Gulp, gulp, gulp, gulp," gurgled Baby Frog.....
"You'll sail away," yelled Mother and Father Frog.
"Gulp, gulp, gulp," gurgled Baby Frog as three more bubbles disappeared.
"You'll grow round as a ball," frowned Mother and Father Frog.
"Gulp, gulp," gurgled Baby Frog as two more bubbles disappeared.
"Your belly will get bigger," said Mother and Father Frog.
"Gulp," gurgled Baby Frog as a bubble disappeared.
"Never gulp at a bubble," sighed Mother Frog as she ate a dragonfly.
As Father Frog grabbed a worm he said," Never gulp at a bubble."

Story Summary

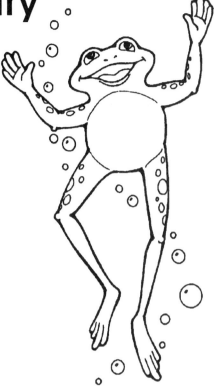

Story Title: _____

Author: _____

Illustrator: _____

After reading the story complete the questions below.

1. Make up a new title for the story.

    _____

2. Give each character a name:

    Mother Frog: _____

    Father Frog: _____

    Baby Frog: _____

3. Write a sentence about your favorite character. _____

    _____

4. What is the problem in the story? Why is Baby Frog so fascinated by bubbles? _____

    _____

5. What happens at the end of the story? How can Baby Frog be helped?

    _____

    BONUS: Change the ending of the story.
    What would happen to Baby Frog in your story?

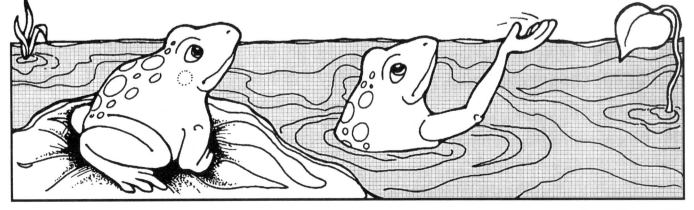

Make Books

How To Make a Wall Book

This is a delightful variation of Big Books for students to make and share with the whole school!

- Group students in small cooperative groups of two, three, or four.
- Divide sentence strips on page 16. Students may use their own handwriting instead of pre-written strips.
- Glue sentence strips to a large sheet of white butcher paper which has been cut into various bubble shapes. Each group is in charge of one sentence strip and illustration.
- Students illustrate each bubble page. They may use finger paints, chalk, crayons, markers, tissue paper, or pieces of construction paper.
- Create a title page by drawing a frog on the front cover. Add title and authors (if dialogue was rewritten by the students, make sure their signatures are included).
- Staple the title page and bubbles on a wall in the hallway or in the library for all students to read and enjoy!

How To Make a Window Book

This versatile book will surely be a double bubble hit as it stirs the thinking process!

Materials:

8 pieces of construction paper (a lesser amount can be used for younger children); magazines; drawing paper; scissors; glue; crayons; stapler

Directions:

1. Number the construction paper pages 1 to 8. Using the bubble pattern on page 19 as a guide, cut a hole the size of circle 1 on the first page, circle 2 on the second, circle 3 on the third, etc. Do not cut a hole on page 8.

2. Glue one large picture or drawing of a bubble scene onto the eighth page.

3. Restack pages from 1 to 8 so smallest window (page 1) is on top.

4. Design a title page around the smallest window.

5. Staple left side of pages to create a window book.

Extensions:

1. For a language arts activity have students add descriptions to each page based on what can be seen through the window.

2. Use the window book as a game. When books are completed, allow students to trade books and try to figure out what the picture is.

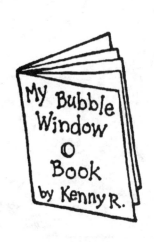

3. List a descriptive word under each window.

18

Window Book Pattern

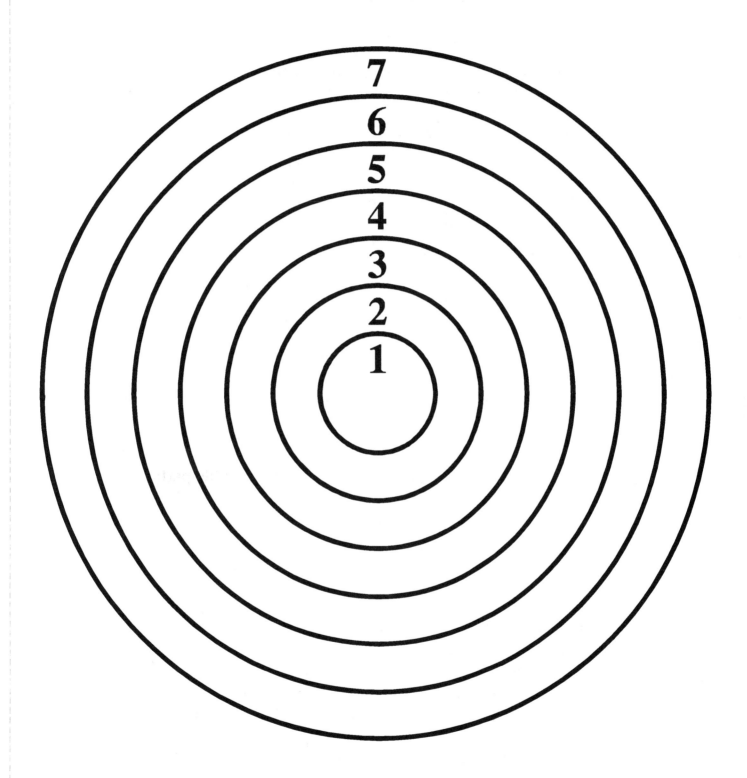

Professor Bubbles' Official Bubble Handbook

by Richard Faverty

Summary

The discovery of the how's and wow's of bubbles are magnificently presented in this handbook. Bubbles are a magical phenomenon to all who come face to face with them, but Professor Bubbles makes the world of bubbles so very tangible that a ripple of excitement will naturally take place.

Inquisitiveness and fascination go hand-in-hand as students explore, experiment, create, design, and discover the whys of bubbles. Professor Bubbles' handbook provides over 90 pages of astonishing bubble science fun! Bubble projects include twin bubbles, the dancing bubble, the bubble twist and many more. Each project will stimulate the use of science, math, creative writing, language arts, and reading. Professor Bubbles' simple directions, photographs and "secret tips" will lead your students from beginner to advanced bubbleology using techniques of breath control, finger dexterity, and fun exploration.

The outline below is a suggested plan for using the various activities that are presented in this unit. You should adapt these ideas to fit your own classroom situation.

Sample Plan

Day I

- Bubble Trivia (page 27)
- Bubble Puzzle (pages 56-57)
- Book Talks (page 12)
- Week of Daily Writings Bubble Activity Cards (page 34)
- Language Arts: Who, What, When, Where of Bubbles (page 48)
- Assign Homework: Design poster (page 22)

Day II

- Bubble Trivia (page 27)
- Bubble science projects-Beginner Level (page 21)
- Tug of Bubbles (page 64).
- Bubble Jumble Sentence Sense (page 47)
- Poetry: The Bubble Pipe (page 45).
- Art: Personalized Bubble Wands (page 67)
- Bubble Pocket Vocabulary (pages 50-51)
- Journal Writing (page 28)

Day III

- Bubble Trivia (page 27)
- Bubble science projects—Intermediate Level (page 21)
- Clothespin Bubble Story (page 49)
- Math: Bubble Count (page 54)
- Creative Writing: Bubble Thoughts (page 33)
- Journal Writing: Write to the author (page 22)

Day IV

- Bubble Trivia (page 27)
- Octopus Riddle Book (pages 30-31)
- Math: Bubble Colors (page 55)
- Hidden Objects (page 52)
- Favorite Bubble Experiment Report (page 35)
- Compile journal writings

Day V

- Culminating Activity: How To Become an "Offiicial Bubbleologist" (pages 69-70)

Overview of Activities

SETTING THE STAGE

1. **Spark** your students' curiosity with a new addition to your Bubbles Learning Center—The Discovery of a Soap Film (page 8). Fill a tray with at least 10 "odds/ends" from home (cheese cutter, egg beater, comb, etc). A demonstration of what a soap film looks like is advisable by performing the Professor's "Bubble Frame Activity" on pages 32-33 for the whole class. Display a checklist with names of the objects (place a drawing of the object for younger children) in one column, a happy bubble face to indicate "yes" if the object will form a soap film in another column, and a sad bubble face to indicate that the object will not form a bubble film in the last column. After all predictions are made, an unveiling of "Soap Film" objects should be demonstrated for all to see. Discuss why objects do or do not form bubble films.

What Objects Form Soapfilms?		
Object Name	☺	☹
paperclip	✓	
hairbrush		✓
rim of cup	✓	
rubberband	✓	
spoon		✓

2. Prepare the groundwork for the making of a filmstrip "How to Become an Official Bubbleologist" by doing a book review of *Professor Bubbles' Official Bubble Handbook.*

   • Write title and author on chalkboard and display the book so all can view it. Have students make predictions about what types of information the bubble book might provide.

   • Help students become familiar with bubble terms by completing Bubble Pocket Vocabulary on pages 50-51.

   • Display an outline that shows the coming attractions of bubble science projects from Professor Bubbles' book. Students will complete these on their journey to becoming an "Official Bubbleologist!"

Beginner Level	Intermediate Level	Advanced Level
a. Basic Bubbles (pages 16-17)	a. Double Bubble (pages 20-21)	a. Bubble Twist (page 47)
b. Bubble Burst (page 26)	b. Bubble in a Bubble (pages 30-31)	b. Bubble Chain (pages 68-69)
c. Bubble Spray (pages 56-57)	c. Bubble Trampoline (page 42)	c. Magic String (page 88)
*Bonus: Bubble Cylinder (page 60)	*Bonus: Giant Bubble (page 44)	*Bonus: Rainbow Bubble (page 82)

Using the book and the posters, discuss the projects and make predictions! Read Bubble Basics on pages 74-77. The experiments listed above are optional. Adapt these or others to your class.

Overview of Activities *(cont.)*

ENJOYING THE BOOK

1. **Homework Activity:** Have students create a poster to advertise their upcoming video film on becoming a bubbleologist. Design and draw a poster which includes information such as title, time, and place. Supply construction paper, butcher paper, poster board, glitter, markers, crayons, paints, glue and stencils. Display posters in hallways! This project could be done in small groups.

2. Read-Explore-Discover bubble science by completing Professor Bubbles' projects. These projects can be done in workable pairs within designated classroom areas.

   - Set up beginning, intermediate, or advanced experiments each day.
   - Prepare instruction sheets for each experiment (page 23). Display at a desirable site.
   - Students complete experiment worksheet (page 24) after each level.
   - Students rate each experiment (page 25). Add the rating sheets to a Bubble Journal!
   - Create a "Bubble Chain" around your room. As students complete each experiment have them fill out a bubble (patterns, page 26). At the end of the day, staple bubbles to make a chain effect. **Goal:** Circle the room with bubbles!

3. Play "Tug of Bubbles" with the whole class. It's an exhilarating game for outdoor fun (page 64).

EXTENDING THE BOOK

1. Write to the author! Professor Bubbles encourages his fellow bubbleologists to write to him. Have your students design their own bubble stationery or use letter form (page 76). Letters can include thoughts, ideas, questions about bubbles; share a new bubble invention; or ask him to visit the school. Here's his address:

   > Professor Bubbles
   > P.O. Box 613
   > Wilmette, Illinois 60091

2. **Culminating Activity:** Your students will be "wound up" as they participate in the making of a video film entitled "How to Become an Official Bubbleologist" (pages 69-70).

3. Have students present reports on their favorite experiments (page 35).

4. Collect your students' "Rate This Experiment" worksheets. Display a bar graph on a board and discover what your class viewed as their favorite versus total flop experiment!

Experiment Instruction Sheet

_____

Name of experiment

BEGINNER   INTERMEDIATE   ADVANCED

Circle one level

Materials needed:

_____ _____ _____

_____ _____ _____

_____ _____ _____

Goal:_____

* Star question to think about:_____

_____

Steps to follow:

1._____

_____

2._____

_____

3._____

_____

4._____

_____

5._____

_____

6._____

_____

Secret tip: _____

Complete experiment worksheet (page 24)!

Bubbleologist Result Sheet

Scientist Name: _____

Directions: Complete the questions below.

1. Use one word to describe how well this experiment went. (Rule: Do not use the word O.K.)

   _____

2. Did you have any problems with the experiment?   (Circle yes or no.)

   Yes   What was (were) the problem(s)?

   _____

   _____

   How did you solve the problem(s)?

   _____

   _____

   No   What did you do to make the experiment go so smoothly?

   _____

   _____

   _____

3. How did the "secret tip" help you? _____

   _____

4. Draw a picture on the back of this page to show what the results of your experiment looked like.

5. Did you discover something "new" about bubbles? Describe.

   _____

Write a new experiment about bubbles on another page. Remember to include materials needed, a title, steps to follow, questions to think about and results. Share with your classmates!

Rate the Experiment

Title of experiment: _____

Scientist(s) name(s): _____

_____

_____

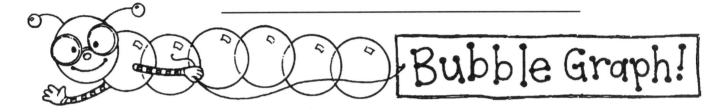

Color the bubblewand bar graph to rate this experiment!

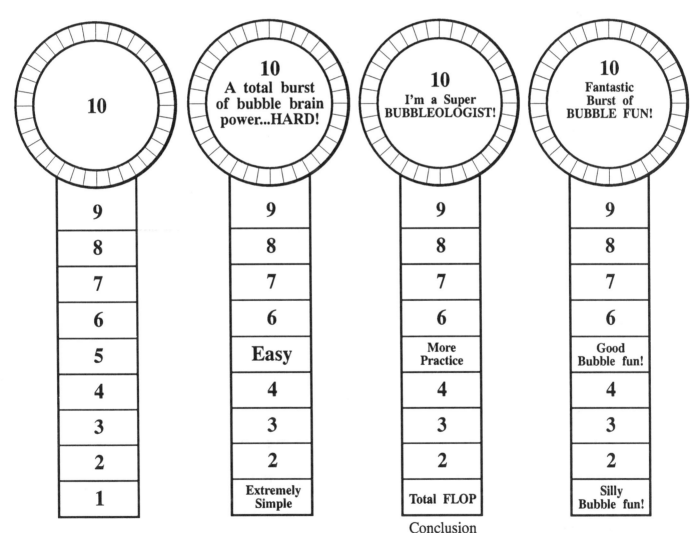

10	**10** A total burst of bubble brain power...HARD!	**10** I'm a Super BUBBLEOLOGIST!	**10** Fantastic Burst of BUBBLE FUN!
9	9	9	9
8	8	8	8
7	7	7	7
6	6	6	6
5	Easy	More Practice	Good Bubble fun!
4	4	4	4
3	3	3	3
2	2	2	2
1	Extremely Simple	Total FLOP	Silly Bubble fun!

Conclusion

How many scientists were in your group? | **How hard was this experiment?** | **How did your experiment end?** | **How much did you like the experiment?**

Bubble Chain

Directions: Have students outline the bubble in one of the colors it changes to (blue, green, purple, yellow, white). Of course, the popped bubbles will be outlined in black!

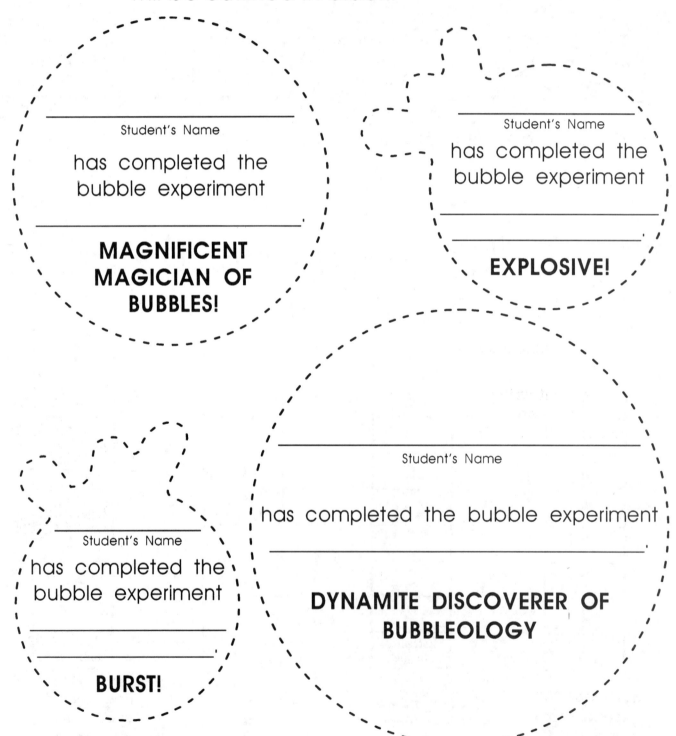

_____
Student's Name

has completed the bubble experiment
_____.

MAGNIFICENT MAGICIAN OF BUBBLES!

_____
Student's Name

has completed the bubble experiment
_____.

EXPLOSIVE!

_____
Student's Name

has completed the bubble experiment
_____.

BURST!

_____
Student's Name

has completed the bubble experiment
_____.

DYNAMITE DISCOVERER OF BUBBLEOLOGY

Daily Writing Activities

Bubbleologist Daily Journal

CERTIFICATE of BUBBLEOLOGY

This is to certify that

_____
student's name

has completed the

beginning • intermediate • advanced

*bubble science projects
magnificently
to become an*

***Official
Bubbleologist***

Your students will surely graduate into the field of Bubbleology as Bubbleologists. Who or what is a "Bubbleologist"? It is a person who studies the sticky, silly, slippery, soapy, colorful science of bubbles. Each student will use a Bubble Journal Worksheet (page 28) for daily writing. Pages can be stored between a folded sheet of decorated paper (Bubble Surprise, page 66). Students add all bubble work to this journal. Staple completed work at the end of the unit.

Keeping daily journals will help students to determine main ideas, find supporting details, summarize, comprehend and synthesize facts and ideas they are learning, and incorporate new vocabulary and concepts into their background knowledge. These opportunities can be especially beneficial to low-achieving students.

Bubble Trivia

Capture your students' attention as they play "bubble trivia." This will be easy to do since questions are designed and written by the students!

1. Design a bubble question box and place it at the Learning Center site.

2. Each student writes one question a day on bubble strips (page 36). It can be a new or review fact about bubbles. Deposit strips into the question box.

3. Start the bubble unit each day with a trivia question.

4. One student chooses a question and reads it aloud.

5. All students record their answers on Bubble Trivia Worksheet (page 37).

6. Discuss answer. Each correct response receives a bubble sticker. (Stickers can be created by tracing the small bubble patterns found on page 72 onto colored sheets of cellophane paper. Cut out. Students may glue bubbles onto worksheet.)

7. **Culminating Activity:** At the end of bubble unit students count bubble stickers and go to "Bubble Store" to buy bubble paraphernalia (student-made bubble books, wands, cans). Teacher determines how many bubble stickers are needed to purchase various bubble items.

Bubbleologist Journal Worksheet

Directions: Write or draw something new you have learned about bubbles today!

Day 1	**Day 2**
    _____ _____ _____	 _____ _____ _____
Day 3	**Day 4**
    _____ _____ _____	 _____ _____ _____

* Write a list of "bubble words" that describe what a bubble feels, smells, or looks like. Add a few words each day.

* Draw a bubble city, a bubble house, or a bubble person.

Add your own bubble pages to the journal.

* Design your own bubble blower.

* Write an imaginative story.

Daily Writing Activities *(cont.)*

Bubble-Toons Flip Book

Lights! Camera! Action! There's no doubt this activity of sharing bubble stories will be a smash hit in your classroom. Students sign up in advance for a special day. For presentations provide a special chair at the front of the room. Have a parent volunteer videotape the sessions.

Preparation:

1. Explain that each student will become an author today.

2. Review or introduce concept of the who, what, or where of a story. Use *Never Snap at a Bubble* as a group example. Allow students to brainstorm who will be in their stories; where the character is going to or coming from; or what type of problem the character will experience.

3. As a total group, discuss the kind of action pictures that will show what's happening to their characters.

4. Encourage the use of descriptive words in their stories by listing words on the board.

Directions:

Fold two pieces of paper (8 1/2" x 11") into 4 squares. (See diagram below.)

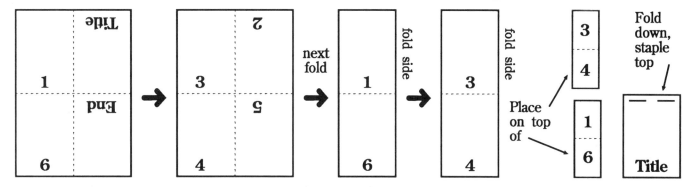

Writing Process:

1. Draw your characters doing somthing different in each square.

2. Draw speaking bubbles in each square.

3. Write what each character is expressing in the speaking bubbles. Make sure it tells a story!

Presentations:

1. Each student reads aloud their character's captions and shares illustrations and their favorite quote.

2. The audience may comment and ask questions about the story.

Daily Writing Activities *(cont.)*

Octopus Riddle Book

Pass out the "ink" and get your students geared up to write riddles. Duplicate one octopus, one cover, and as many arms as are needed for each student. (See pages 30 and 31 for patterns.)

1. Cut out the pages.

2. Write a riddle question on the front of the blank page. Then write the answer on the back. Draw a picture for added excitement! Make as many pages as you wish.

3. Color and cut out octopus and cover.

4. Staple pages to octopus with a cover on top.

5. Glue to a piece of colored construction paper for added durability.

6. Share your riddle book with a friend!

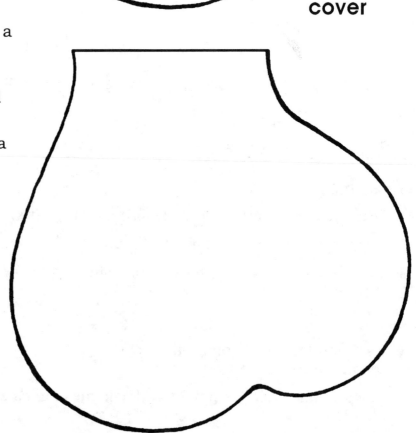

cover

page

30

Octopus Riddle Book

Bubbles Magically Escape

Materials: construction paper (8 ½" x 11" / 22 x 28cm), scissors, glue, crayons or markers, stapler

Preparation: Duplicate this page for each student. Have them color and cut it out. Glue it onto construction paper. Use it as a cover for their story.

Silly-slippery-soapy bubbles are coming out of your bathtub! Write a funny story about this situation. Who put the soap in the water pipes?

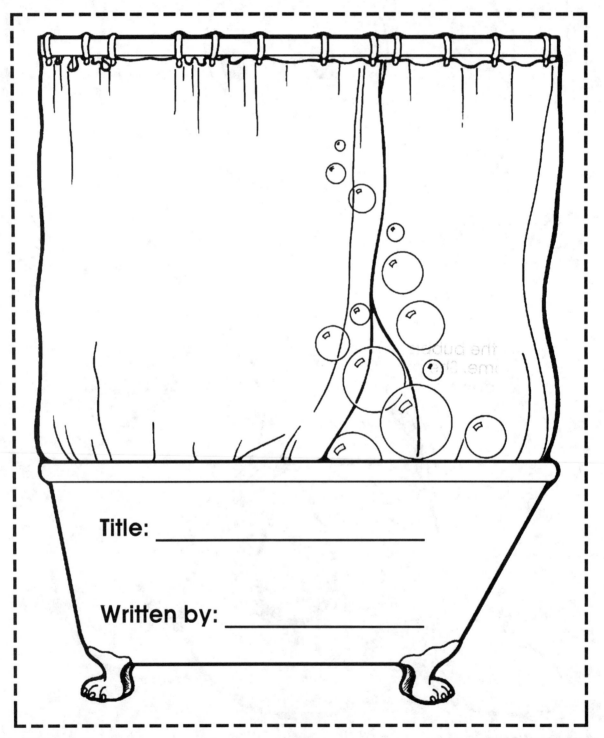

Title: _____

Written by: _____

Bubble Thoughts

Directions:

1. Fold an 8'' (20cm) square piece of construction paper into four square sections.

2. Write what the robot might be saying inside each speech bubble below.

3. Cut the cartoons out and glue to the construction paper in the correct order.

4. Share your robot cartoon with a friend!

#275 Thematic Unit — Bubbles

Bubble Activity Cards

Directions: Laminate cards below. Cut apart. Use at Learning Center for independent or group work.

Activity 1	Activity 4
How many words can you discover in ``SUPER BUBBLEOLOGIST?'' Write a list. Challenge a partner. Who can find the most bubble words? ***Use your dictionary.**	Use your dictionary to find the word bubble. What are the guide words on that page? How many syllables are in the word bubble? Find other words that end in ``ble.''
Activity 2	**Activity 5**
Design a T-shirt to advertise your authentic bubble solution. Give your bubble solution a name!	A villain has stolen the last bubble pet in the world and has blasted off to the moon. How will you get the bubble pet back? Write a short story.
Activity 3	**Activity 6**
Write a letter to your aunt, uncle, cousin, or a friend and tell them all the new facts you've learned about bubbles!	It is your birthday and you have asked your mom for a ``bubble cake''! Write a recipe for her to follow. Make sure you list all the ingredients.

     34

Favorite Bubble Experiment Report

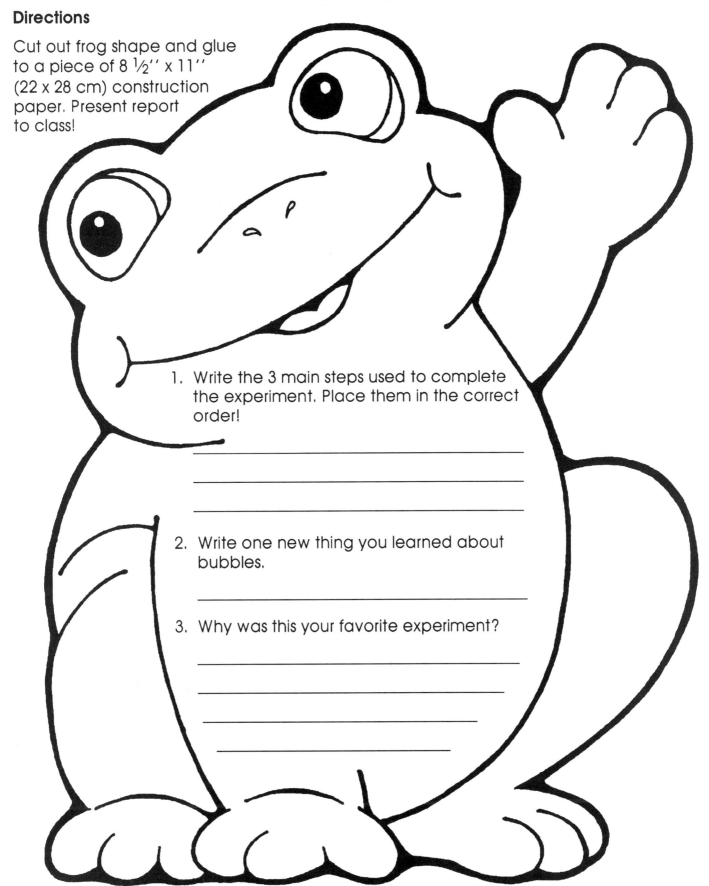

Directions

Cut out frog shape and glue to a piece of 8 ½'' x 11'' (22 x 28 cm) construction paper. Present report to class!

1. Write the 3 main steps used to complete the experiment. Place them in the correct order!

   _____

   _____

   _____

2. Write one new thing you learned about bubbles.

   _____

3. Why was this your favorite experiment?

   _____

   _____

   _____

   _____

Bubble Strips

BUBBLEOLOGIST NAME: _____

QUESTION: _____

_____

_____

• **WRITE ANSWER ON BACK** •

TIP: Make sure your sentences are complete. Ask a friend to check.

BUBBLEOLOGIST NAME: _____

QUESTION: _____

_____

_____

• **WRITE ANSWER ON BACK** •

TIP: Make sure your sentences are complete. Ask a friend to check.

BUBBLEOLOGIST NAME: _____

QUESTION: _____

_____

_____

• **WRITE ANSWER ON BACK** •

TIP: Make sure your sentences are complete. Ask a friend to check.

BUBBLEOLOGIST NAME: _____

QUESTION: _____

_____

_____

• **WRITE ANSWER ON BACK** •

TIP: Make sure your sentences are complete. Ask a friend to check.

Name ______________________________

Bubble Trivia Worksheet

1. ______________________________
____

2. ______________________________
____

3. ______________________________
____

4. ______________________________
____

5. ______________________________
____

6. ______________________________
____

7. ______________________________
____

8. ______________________________
____

9. ______________________________
____

10. ______________________________
____

Bobbin' Bubbles

This poetry mini-unit can be used any time during the Bubbles Unit. If preferred, single activities from this mini-unit can be incorporated into your bubble studies.

1. Duplicate the Bobbin' Bubble Poem below on chart paper or chalkboard for all students to see. Define **simile**. (It is a comparison between two unrelated things using the words **as** or **like**.) Have students find the simile and copy it.

2. Have students read in unison with rhythm, voice intonation, and giggly fun! They might even enjoy acting like bobbin' bubbles.

Bobbin' Bubbles

Bubbles... bubbles are

Slippery and smooth

Bobbin' and bouncing

Silly as kangaroos

Bubbles...bubbles in the air!

3. Brainstorm with class. Develop a Bubble Word Bank on an overhead projector or chalkboard.

Bubble Word Bank			
Descriptive Words	**Action Words**	**Places Found**	**Similes**
purple	popping	in sodas	light as a feather
wet	flying	near fish	clear as glass
shiny	floating	by scuba divers	round as an orange

4. Make a large chart of the worksheet on page 41. With the whole class, model filling in the blanks with the words from the Bubble Word Bank.

5. Group students in workable pairs. Have them create and illustrate their own simile poem using worksheet on page 41. They may use words from the Bubble Bank or make up their own.

Poems

Descriptive Poems

These poems can be written by small cooperative groups of 3-4 or individually. Get students involved by allowing them to blow and chew bubble gum. Provide one piece of wrapped gum to each member of the group and four index cards or strips of construction paper per group. Each strip will be labeled as follows:

_____ bubblegum.

1. Each member of the group chews and blows bubbles.

2. They think of descriptive words that describe the gum (snappy, stretchy).

3. Assign one member of each group to be the recorder and record all the words that are associated with the gum chewing. Choose the best four to put on the strips.

4. When finished, glue strips onto a sheet of large construction paper to have a completed poem. Give it a title.

5. Investigate the most common sound words used in each group. Display a large bar graph on chalkboard or overhead projector.

6. Complete the worksheet (page 44) for further descriptive writing experience.

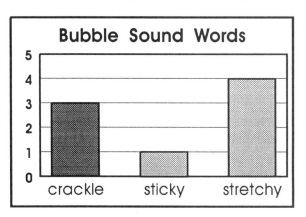

Bub-lets

Provide the first line of a bub-let or two line rhyming poem. Then brainstorm words that rhyme with the last word in the line. Together the class can create a second line. Pair the students and have them write and illustrate their own bubble gum wrappers with a bub-let poem inside.

Sample First Lines

Bubbles sparkle up the sky...

Two tiny bubbles caught by a frog...

Soda pop bubbles tickled my nose...

Bubblegum bubble splats over my face...

*Create your own first liners for a bub-let poem.

Art Activities for Poetry

Bubble Jar Labels

Have students create and design authentic bubble labels for their bottled bubbleologist bubble solution.

1. Provide blank name tag stickers.

2. Use colorful thin-point markers and design the border of the tag.

3. Use alliteration (the repetition of the initial sound in two or more words) for inside the border.

Benjamin's Blue Bubbles

name of
student

Bubble Dyes

Have students work in pairs for this activity.

1. Add food coloring to a jar of "Bubbleologist Bubble Solution." Students will have to experiment with the amount of food coloring.

2. Blow bubbles with a bubble wand. NOTE: If this activity is done indoors, it is advisable to use a paint tarp or newspapers.

3. Catch bubbles on sheets of white construction paper. Let dry!

4. Complete by writing a Name Poem (a name written vertically and each line of poetry begins with a letter in that word) on the "splotches" of bubbles.

5. Display for all to enjoy!

Bouncing Bubbles
Up
Beyond the
Blue Sky
Like a balloon
Exploding

Bobbin' Bubble Worksheet

Directions   With a partner write a bubble simile poem. Illustrate it in the bubble frame below!

Written and illustrated by:

_____

_____ **BUBBLES**

Bubbles . . . . . bubbles are

_____ and _____
descriptive word   descriptive word

and _____
action word   action word

_____ as _____
simile

Bubbles . . . . . bubbles _____.
place

Bubble Square Dance

A ripply, rainbow bubble went up for a glance

On a bright spring day.

(Form circle with left hand thumb and forefinger)

It swirled and whirled about to the windman's song—

(Both arms sway overhead)

Sail away—sail away—sail away—

Up over the clouds,

Down above the trees.

(Both arms swing low)

It rollicked and frolicked with the birds in flight

Till a meadow of flowers came into sight.

Music billowed up on waves of air.

A fairy clan do-sie-doed below.

The bubble swooped down to join the fun.

But an itsy bitsy gnome spotted it in the sun.

(Make glasses from fingers; place around eyes.)

No time for a bubble square dance or two;

A sharp pointed gnome finger gave it a pinch.

And pop!

(Clap!)

The ripply, rainbow bubble disappeared from sight!

(Hands behind back.)

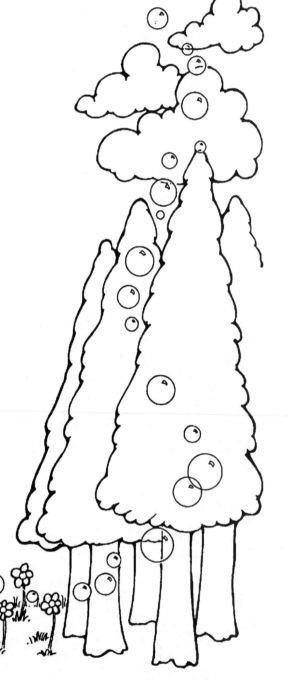

42

Bubble Square Dance Activities

1. Brainstorm the who, what, when, and why of the poem's title before reading the poem to the class. Write responses on chalkboard. Read the poem, stopping when you get to "But an itsy bitsy gnome spotted it...". Have students close their eyes and imagine what will the little elf do! Have students draw what they think will happen and write a complete sentence to explain. Then come back to story circle and read the ending of the poem. Have fun sharing everyone's creative picture and ending. Display drawings for all to see!

2. Display poem on a large piece of poster board and recite the poem together as a class.

3. Learn body and hand movements to the poem on page 42.

4. Write the poem on sentence strips. Use as a learning center activity.

5. Make a "Bubble Fairy" stick puppet. Students will engage in laughter and giggles as the Bubble Fairy joins them in reciting the Bubble Square Dance (page 42).

6. Transform the poem's verses into a delightful story by following directions on page 18 for a wall book.

7. Have a Bubble Square Dance Play presentation:

   * Assign small group of students to be script writers, prompt makers, bubbledancers, or fairy folk.

   * Students can be assigned to be the itsy bitsy gnome, the bubble that pops, or the narrator of the play.

   * Perform the play at a bubble party for other classes to enjoy or at a nursing home visit!

Name _____

Onomatopoeia Poetry

Directions: Write a poem about sounds that things make. Don't forget a sound title! Read finished poem to members of your group. Illustrate your favorite sound on another sheet of paper. Use your imagination and listen to the sounds!

_____
Sound Title

Snapping _____ bubble gum.

Bubbles **pop** _____.

_____ teapot.

Sausage _____.

_____ bells.

Rollerskates _____.

_____ kites.

Balloons _____.

_____ kids.

44

The Bubble Pipe

Directions: Write a bubble shape poem about a bubble pipe. When you are finished, read your poem to a friend!

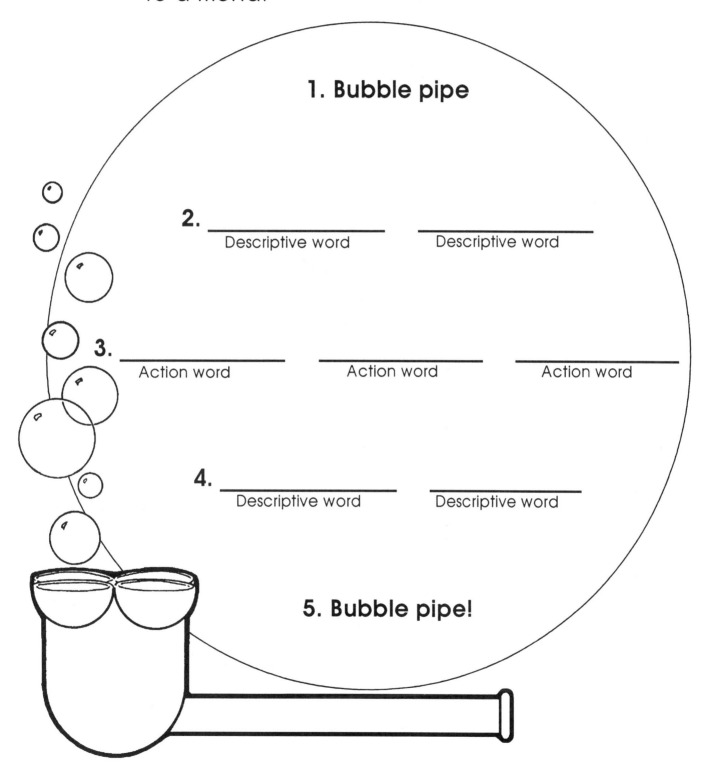

1. Bubble pipe

2. _____   _____
   Descriptive word   Descriptive word

3. _____   _____   _____
   Action word   Action word   Action word

4. _____   _____
   Descriptive word   Descriptive word

5. Bubble pipe!

The Deep Dive for Rhyming

Directions: Name each bubble. Make each name rhyme with "snap."

BONUS: Write a sentence using one or more of the rhyming words above.

_____

_____

_____

Bubble Jumble Sentence Sense

Directions: The words in each worm are mixed-up. Put the words in order to make sense. Write the sentences; use the correct punctuation(!?.).

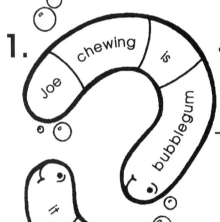

1. chewing is Joe bubblegum

1. _____

_____

2. it what time is

2. _____

_____

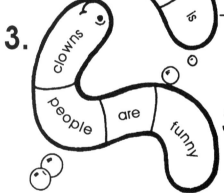

3. clowns people are funny

3. _____

_____

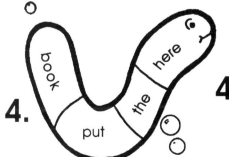

4. book here the put

4. _____

_____

Who, What, When, Where of Bubbles

Directions: Read the words in the bubble soda bottle. Write the words in correct bubble who-what-when-where category!

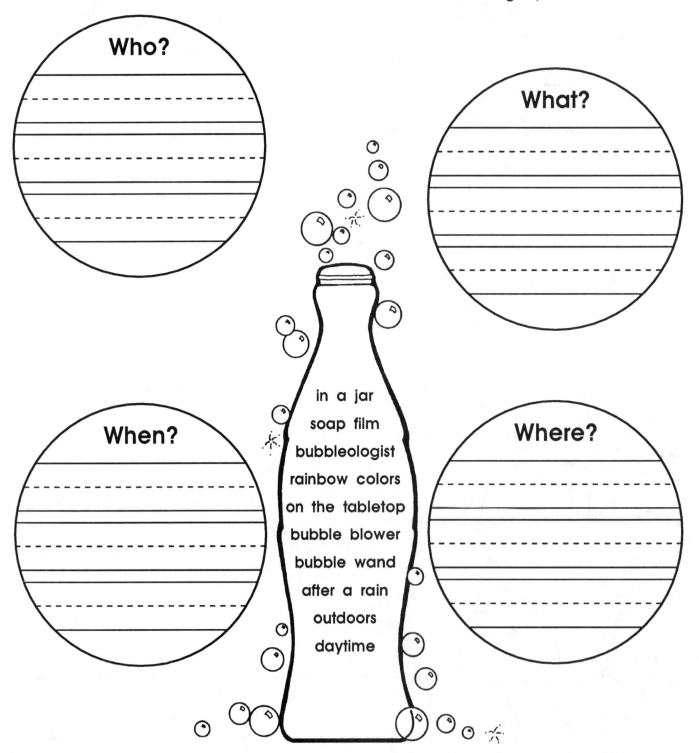

Who?

What?

When?

Where?

in a jar
soap film
bubbleologist
rainbow colors
on the tabletop
bubble blower
bubble wand
after a rain
outdoors
daytime

Clothespin Bubble Story

Materials:

7 clothespins; tagboard; envelope; glue

Preparation:

1. Write answers on clothespins.
2. Make a pocket envelope on back of story.
3. Mount the picture story below on tagboard. Laminate for durability.
4. Cut out answer key (page 79) and store in back pocket for students to self correct!

Directions:

Read the story, snap clothespin answer onto correct bubble.

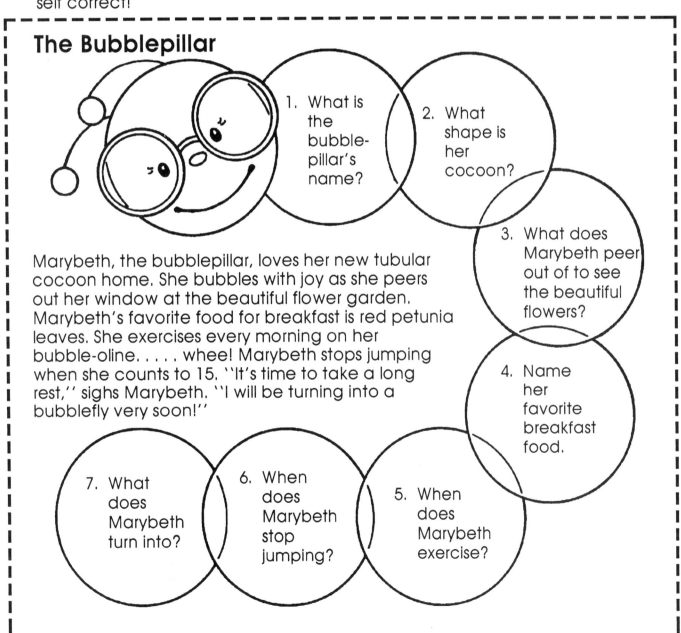

The Bubblepillar

1. What is the bubble-pillar's name?

2. What shape is her cocoon?

3. What does Marybeth peer out of to see the beautiful flowers?

4. Name her favorite breakfast food.

Marybeth, the bubblepillar, loves her new tubular cocoon home. She bubbles with joy as she peers out her window at the beautiful flower garden. Marybeth's favorite food for breakfast is red petunia leaves. She exercises every morning on her bubble-oline. . . . . whee! Marybeth stops jumping when she counts to 15. ``It's time to take a long rest,'' sighs Marybeth. ``I will be turning into a bubblefly very soon!''

5. When does Marybeth exercise?

6. When does Marybeth stop jumping?

7. What does Marybeth turn into?

Bubble Pocket Vocabulary

Directions:

1. Cut out Bubblesaurus (page 50) and glue to construction paper.

2. Cut out bubble jars (page 51). Glue around three edges and attach to Bubblesaurus arms.

3. Cut out vocabulary strips (page 51). Read the words. If you know what the word says, place in "I Know" pocket; if not, place in "I'm Learning" pocket.

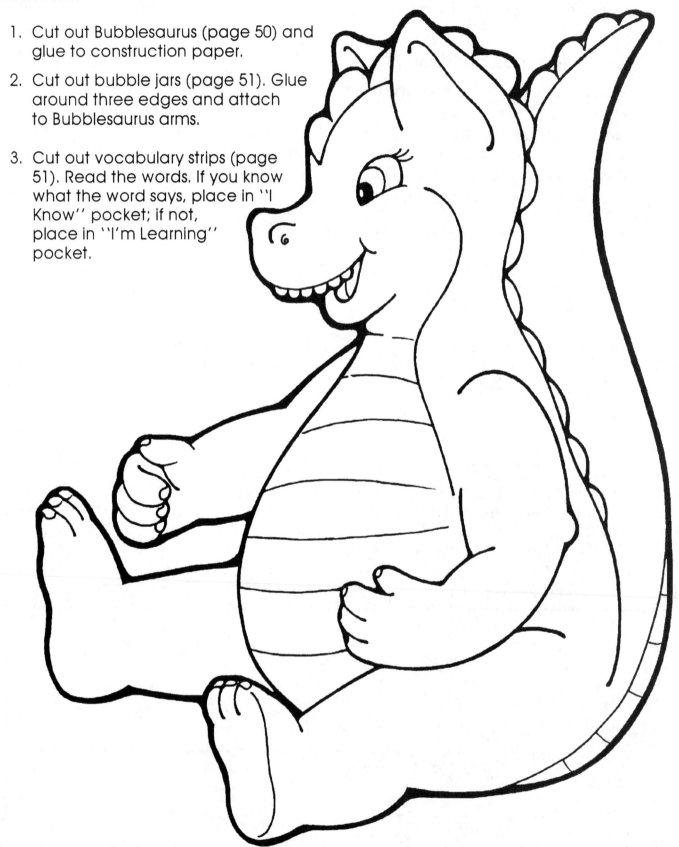

50

Pocket Vocabulary *(cont.)*

Bubble
Words I
Know

Bubble
Words
I'm
Learning

bubble wand	dipping	domes
bubbleologist	bubble frame	straw
soap film	fragile	chain bubbles
evaporate	glycerine	breath control
pop	round	bubble tail
surface tension	distilled water	shake
blow	gentle	patience
Try these skills: put words in ABC order; write a sentence using the words; tell how many syllables in each word; add more vocabulary words you are learning in this bubble unit!		

Hidden Objects

Directions: Bubble-osaurus has lost his tools in a terrible bubble storm. Help him find a **bubble wand**, **jar of bubbles**, **bubble pipe**, **hot air balloon**, and **hat**. Color the lost items!

BONUS: List the lost objects in alphabetical (ABC) order on the back!

The Longest Frog Race

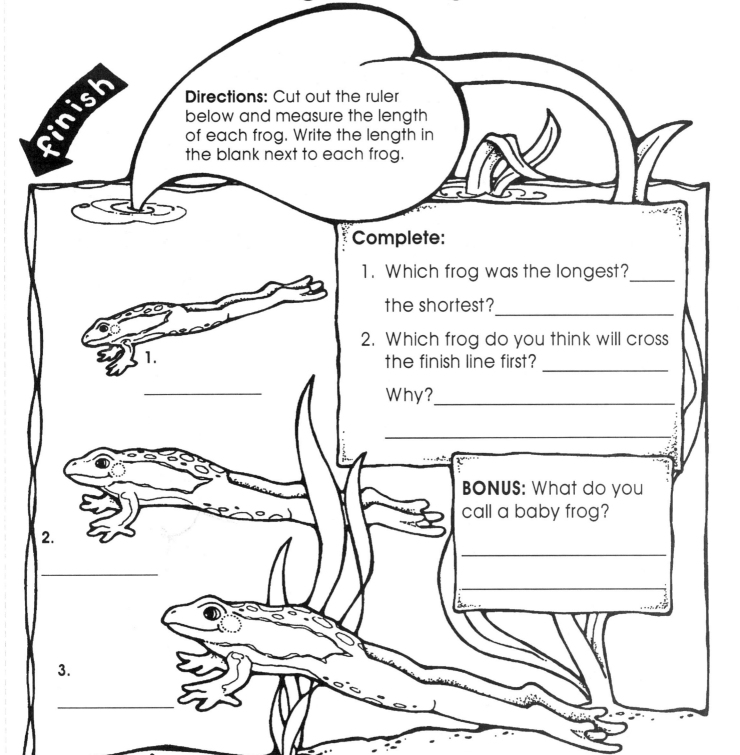

Directions: Cut out the ruler below and measure the length of each frog. Write the length in the blank next to each frog.

finish

1. _____

2. _____

3. _____

Complete:

1. Which frog was the longest?_____

   the shortest?_____

2. Which frog do you think will cross the finish line first? _____

   Why?_____

   _____

BONUS: What do you call a baby frog?

_____

_____

inches
centimeters

17 16 15 14 13 12 11 10 9 8 7 6 5 4 3 2 1 0

0   1   2   3   4   5   6   7

Bubble Count

Directions:

1. You will need 20 small beans, round candies, or coins.

2. Read, follow directions, and answer the questions below.

1. Place 5 beans on Jen.

    Place 8 beans on Kino.

    Place 7 beans on Bub.

    a. Which of these 3 fish has the "least" amount of beans?

    _____

    b. Which fish has the "most" amount of beans?

    _____

    c. If Kino and Bub put their beans together, how many beans would they have?(Do not move counters.)

    _____

    d. If Jen took 3 beans from Bub, how many beans would she have?

    _____

    e. Bub would only have _____ beans left!

2. Outline the new fish named Pat with a crayon.

    a. Pat doesn't have any beans. So Jen, Kino and Bub gave Pat 3 beans from each of their piles. How many beans does Pat have?

    _____

    How many beans does each fish have left?

    _____ Jen _____ Kino _____ Bub

Bubble Colors

One of the most awesome characteristics of bubbles is their colors. When light bounces off the walls of a bubble, we see a rainbow of colors.

Solve the problems in the Bubbles. Find the answer in the code box below and color the bubbles.

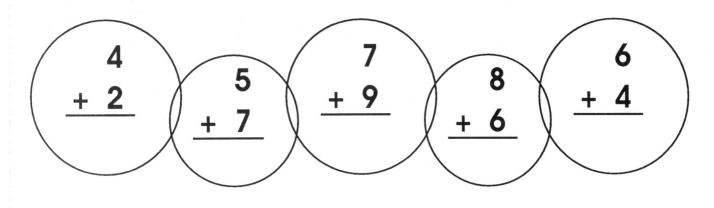

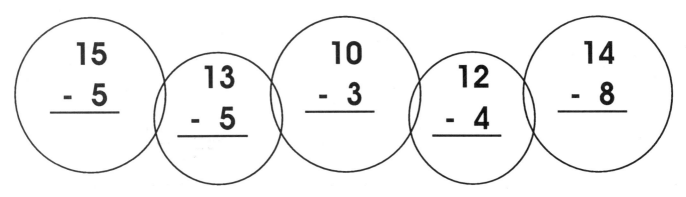

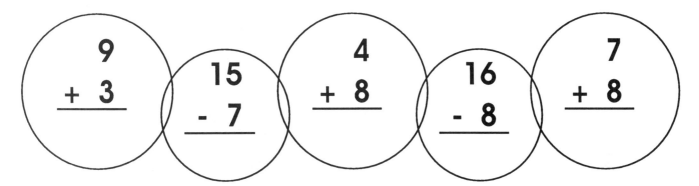

Color Code:

6 = blue	8 = pink	12 = purple	15 = orange
7 = blue/green	10 = yellow	14 = red	16 = green

Bubble Puzzle

Directions:

Reproduce puzzle pieces (page 57). Have students color and cut out. Find the answers on the puzzle pieces and complete the puzzle to discover the mystery picture.

(For use in learning center reproduce onto tagboard, color, and laminate.)

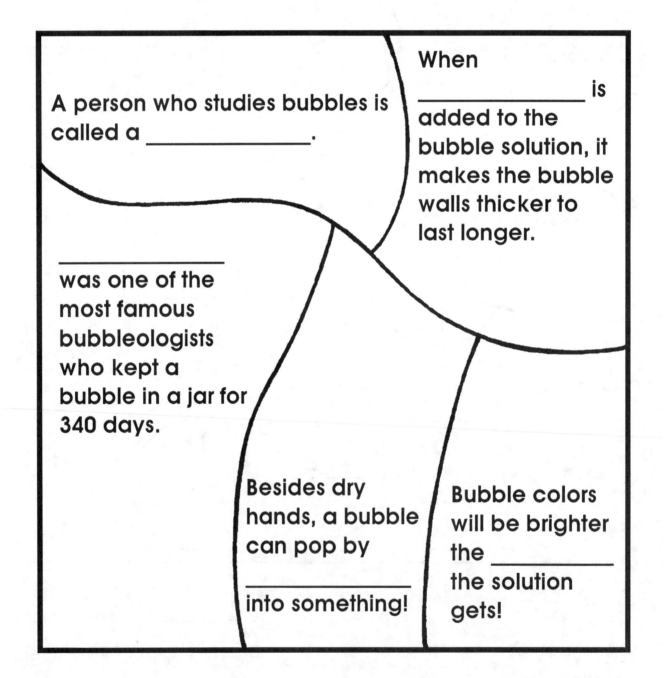

A person who studies bubbles is called a _____.

When _____ is added to the bubble solution, it makes the bubble walls thicker to last longer.

_____ was one of the most famous bubbleologists who kept a bubble in a jar for 340 days.

Besides dry hands, a bubble can pop by _____ into something!

Bubble colors will be brighter the _____ the solution gets!

Bubble Puzzle (cont.)

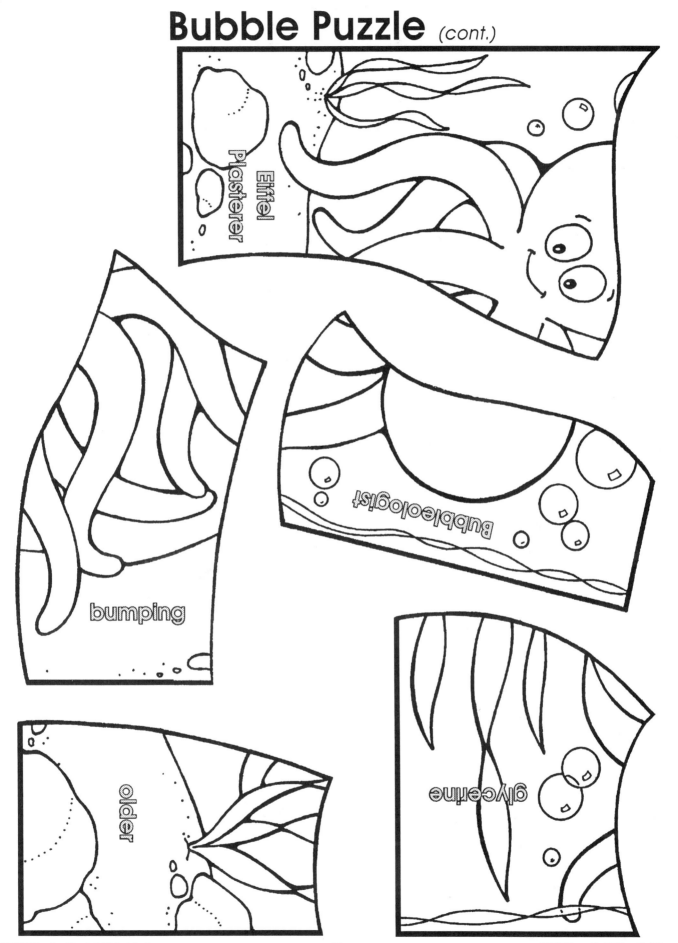

Name _____

News on Bubbles

Directions: Find out some new facts about bubbles. You will be amazed! Cut the words out below. Match and glue them to the correct sentence.

1. Bubble films are like [_____] because they reflect colors.

2. Swirly colors [_____] and change on bubble films.

3. Bubbles blown on flat surfaces are called [_____]

4. Bubbles blown in the air are always [_____] no matter what shape bubble blower you use.

5. Never catch a bubble with a [_____], it wil pop!

6. Once a bubble lived [_____] inside a jar.

mirrors	move	domes
round	dry hand	340 days

The Bubble Gameboard

Color, cut out, and glue gameboard to the inside of a file folder. Then cut out the directions (page 60) and glue to the back of the file folder. Cut apart the task cards (page 60). Store in an envelope attached to the back of the file folder. Have one or several students design the cover. Laminate the file folder and task cards for durability.

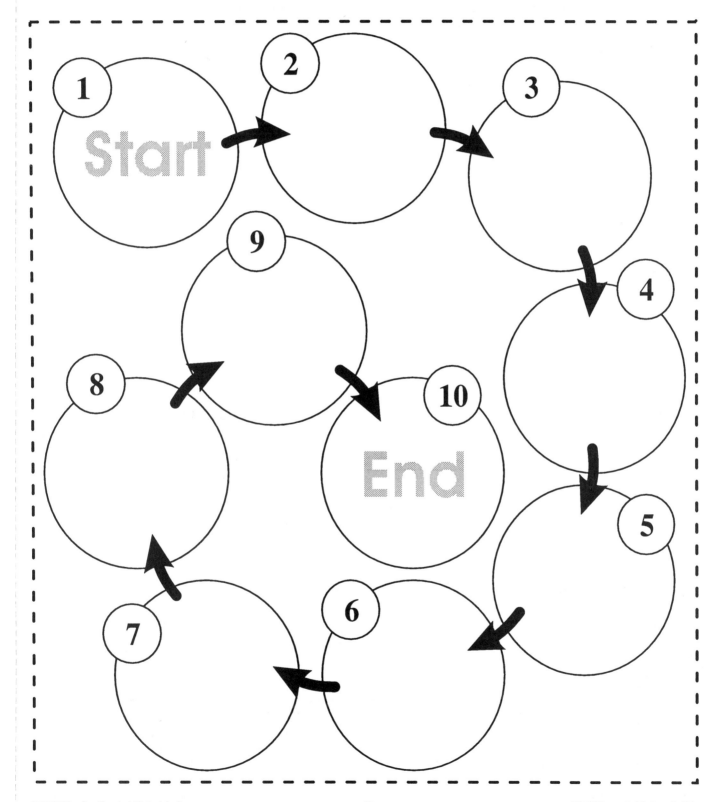

Bubble Gameboard *(cont.)*

Directions: This game is for 2-4 players. Or, two teams of two players each may play. Teams act as one player but they can determine an answer together. Each player will need a marker. Use a die or spinner that has only ones or twos on it.

1. Place the task cards in a pile.
2. Take a task card and answer the question.
3. If you answer correctly, roll the die or spinner and move that many spaces.
4. If you answer incorrectly, stay on the same space.
5. The first player on the team to reach the end wins.

Task Cards

Use these or make your own. Have books available so students may research answers they do not know. To make this game self-correcting, number each card. Write answer (see page 79) next to the corresponding number on a separate sheet of paper.

1. What is inside a bubble?	10. How does a bubble feel?
2. What colors are seen in a bubble?	11. Do bubbles have tails? Where?
3. What shape is a bubble blown from a wand?	12. Name a word that rhymes with bubble.
4. What makes a bubble move?	13. When is the ''perfect'' time to blow bubbles?
5. Are all bubbles the same size? Why?	14. What shapes are bubbles on a flat surface?
6. How do you touch a bubble without breaking it?	15. What do you call a person who studies bubbles?
7. Name two ingredients in a bubble solution.	16. Name a place where bubbles can be found.
8. How do bubbles taste?	17. How many syllables are in the word bubble?
9. What does it mean when a bubble is ''black''?	18. Use the word bubble in a complete sentence.

Bubble Patterns

What Do I Want to Learn and Observe?

Bubbles blown in the air seem to be all round shape. What happens when bubbles are blown on a flat surface?

Materials: a drinking straw; bubble solution; a table top or tray

* Use a sponge to wet the surface with the soapy solution.

* Dip one end of straw in solution. Hold straw near wet surface; then blow gently through straw. (Hint: Use a can with both ends cut out for big domes.)

* Observe. Are you amazed at the results?

Activity

1. What did you observe?_____

   _____

2. What shapes do they form? _____

   _____

3. Do these bubbles pop easily? _____

   _____

4. Can you make the patterns below?

Number of bubbles in pattern	Can you make these patterns?	How many other patterns can you make with the same number of bubbles? (Draw them.)
2		
3		
4		
5		

Other Bubbles

Did you know that using soap is not the only way to make bubbles? Bubbles can be made in other ways. Here are some ways to make them.

Air Bubbles

Materials:

Glasses; water; tight fitting cover for the glass

Directions:

Fill the glass with water almost to the top. Cover it, making sure no air can get in it. Check your glass in about 2 1/2 hours. There will be bubbles inside the glass. These are air bubbles.

Bubbles and Balloons

Materials:

One balloon per two students; water in a large container such as a bucket

Directions:

Work with a partner. One partner blows up the balloon, holding the top tightly together, so no air escapes. The other partner pushes the balloon under the water. When the balloon is fully submerged, the first partner opens the top of the balloon and lets the air out. You will see bubbles escaping from the balloon. These bubbles are air. Since air is lighter than water, the air rises as bubbles.

Bubbles in Cooking

Bubbles play an important role in cooking. The bubbles that form as a batter of a cake heats up make a cake rise.

Make pancakes with your class. Use your own recipe or a prepared mix. Review the ingredients with the students, explaining that the baking powder, liquid, and heat cause a chemical reaction. Students can see this reaction in the bubbles that appear as the pancakes cook. Have them observe the pancakes and draw a picture of what happens to the pancakes as they get hotter.

     62

Bubble Pet

How long can bubbles ''survive'' in a jar? Do the bubbles last longer in a dark or lighted place? Do this experiment and see.

Materials: 1 small jar (4-8 oz.) with lid, 1 drinking straw, 1 teaspoon bubble solution brewed in class (recipe, page 68)

Directions:

1. Add 1 teaspoon of bubble solution to each jar (do one jar at a time). Slush solution around so there are no dry spots in jar.

2. Dunk one end of straw in the bubble solution then place in jar. You are READY!

3. Hold straw **just a little** off the bottom...blow gently and smoothly...until bubbles fill the jar.

4. Put lid on immediately. Repeat steps 1-3 for the second jar.

5. Place one jar in a dark place and the other in a lighted spot.

6. Write down the changes you see. Make sure you check every 15 minutes, then every ½ hour, and later every hour!

Complete

1. What happened when you blew into the jar? _____

2. Were the bubbles all round shape? _____

   If not, what shapes did you see? _____

3. Complete this bar graph:

   How long did the bubbles last in the jar?

   Circle the one you will use: **minutes**

   hours

   days

   Choose a color for color code: ☐ ☐
   Dark Jar   Light Jar

   Dark Jar   Light Jar

4. Which bubble jar survived the longest? _____

   Why do you think it did? _____

Tug of Bubbles

Object of Game:

To get as many bubbles over the finish line in two minutes (adjustable time frame) as possible.

How To's:

* Designate a starting and finish line (use wide masking tape).

* The distance between the two lines should be no more than 15 feet.

* Divide class into two teams. Have each team decide team name (Bubblemania, Bubble Twisters, Bubble Blasters).

* A scorekeeper (parent, volunteer, or teacher aide) and referee (teacher) are needed.

* Determine ahead of time how many "bubble rounds" will be completed.

* One team stands behind starting line. The other team is on the side lines. The team up to play chooses one person to be the bubble blower. The bubble blower begins blowing bubbles when the referee sounds the whistle. Bubble blower continues blowing bubbles until the end of the bubble round (2 minutes).

* Three team members begin blowing, fanning with their hands, huffing, puffing, or anything to get a bubble over the finish line. Once a team member gets his/her bubble across the finish line next team member is up (only three team members at a time avoids confusion). If a team member's bubble POPS on the way to the finish line, he/she must go to the end of the line. Scorekeeper tallies the bubbles that make it over the finish line. Referee will blast the whistle when time is up. Side line team is up next.

BONUS: If a bubble makes it across the finish line by itself, scorekeeper is to count it as a "free-bie" bubble!

* Winning team is the one with the most bubbles over finish line after designated amount of bubble rounds!

Bubble Fairy Stick Puppet

Directions:

1. **Color** the fairy.

2. **Glue** glitter to her wings. Let dry.

3. **Cut** fairy out.

4. **Staple** fairy to craft stick.

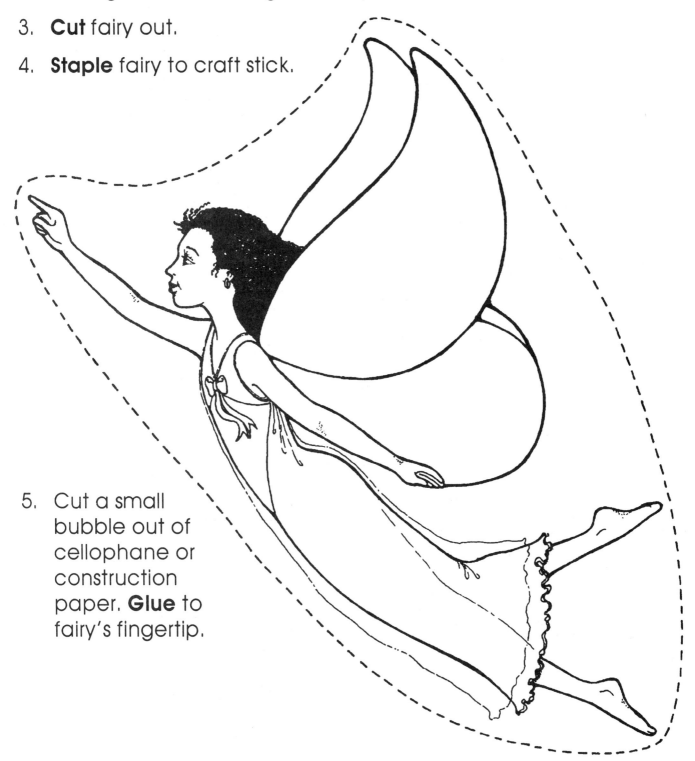

5. Cut a small bubble out of cellophane or construction paper. **Glue** to fairy's fingertip.

Bubble Art Projects

Bubble Surprise

Splish! Splash! Pop! Students will discover creative splotches of color and fun as they engage in catching "paint bubbles."

Materials:

Various colors of poster or tempera paint; $\frac{1}{4}$ cup measuring cup; $\frac{1}{2}$ gallon bubbleologist bubble solution; large bubble wand (6-12 inches); tagboard or white construction paper.

Mix $\frac{1}{4}$ cup of desired color paint into bubble solution (add more for darker color). Divide class into small groups. Each group goes to a parent volunteer or teacher aide who blows colored bubbles. The students try to catch the bubbles on the paper. When the bubbles break, they leave a spectacular array of colored splotches. After everyone catches some bubbles, rotate to next group. (Be sure students wear paint shirts and a paint tarp is laid down for protection.) Finished project becomes the cover of each student's journal!

Bubble Collage

The "Wonderful World of Bubbles" can be captured in this activity. Students, with encouragement of parents, search through old magazines for objects that would make bubbles (old comb, rubber band, etc) or brainstorm a list of where bubbles would be found. Cut out a shape of a bubble blower; then glue to a piece of large colored construction or butcher paper. Glue the pictures, objects, and words about bubbles inside the wand portion.

Floating Frog

Blop! Flop! Hop! into a bucket of water. Students will burst with laughter as they watch their "floating frogs."

Materials Needed:

1" foam balls cut in half; green or brown pipe cleaners cut in half; green/brown tempera paint; small hard beans

Assemble by following illustration.

1. Paint foam dome shape green with brown spots.

2. Bend pipe cleaners and push into foam.

3. Glue on desired color bean for eyes.

66

Personalized Bubble Wands

Materials: Hanger; three feet cotton string; pliers; scissors

Directions:

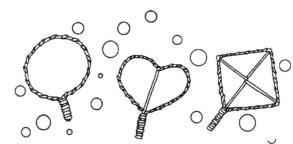

1.   Refer to pages 72-85 of Professor Bubbles' Handbook for basic bubble shape wands.

2.   Think of a bubble shape wand you would like to build.

3.   Draw the bubble shape below. Use your imagination! You may become a new inventor of bubble wands!

4.   Now you are ready to use the materials to create a wand.

5.   Try it out in some bubble solution.

Create a Bubble Solution

Materials:

Glycerine (optional); Dawn or Joy liquid dish soap; measuring cups; water; containers with lids (gallon size)

Ingredients:

1 gallon water; 1 cup Dawn or Joy liquid soap (other soaps will work, but not as well); 40-60 drops of glycerine.

Directions:

Add above ingredients together and stir well. Let solution stand for a week or longer. **Aging the bubble solution allows thicker soap films.**

Activities:

1. Have each student copy recipe on index cards. For added fun glue cards on bubble-shaped cellophane paper. Add the recipe to their bubble journals.

2. Divide students into groups to formulate, measure, and create their bubble solution. Make sure tabletops are covered with newspaper.

3. As a whole class do a compare/contrast graph on:

   a. Aged solution vs. non-aged solution

   b. Glycerine solution vs. non-glycerine solution

Bubble Lollipops

Have your students do an observation of "air bubbles" in lollipops. Buy a variety of lollipops. Make a bar graph to show which brand had the most bubbles. Ask why air gets trapped in the lollipops. Then enjoy the objects of your observation!

How To Become an "Official Bubbleologist"

Take 1! Take 2! Action! will become common words as students engage in making a video about becoming a bubbleologist. Invite parents, other classrooms, and the principal to join in the bubble debut. Serve some ice cream topped with bubblegum while enjoying the film. Then as a bubble finale, hand out the student's official bubbleologist diplomas!

* Students can write their own bubblegrams or use the invitation form on page 77.

Join the Celebration!

What: _____
_____
Where: _____
_____
When: _____
_____

* The making of a video will entail breaking your class into small cooperative groups (prop crew, narrators, camera crew, and the characters). Have your students brainstorm what type of information they want in their film, the scenery, the characters, etc.

* Getting Ready! Some suggested activities for each group are listed below. Add your own creative ideas!

* Get Set! Roll 'em! The camera crew will begin the filming by taking shots of the narrator wearing the introduction poster and begin reading the written script. The narrator will then read some bubble trivia facts, bubble poems, or stories students have written throughout the bubble unit (use several narrators). Try reading a different bubble poem or story before each scene!

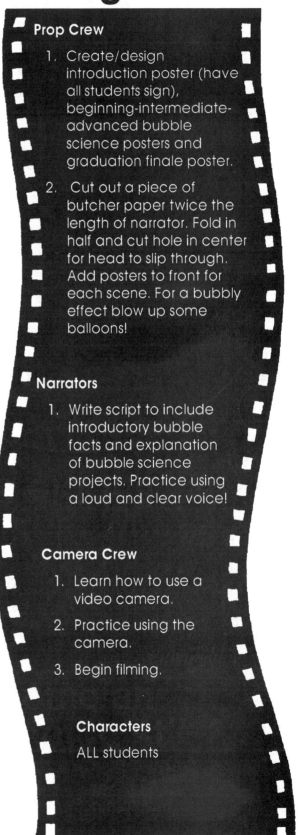

Prop Crew

1. Create/design introduction poster (have all students sign), beginning-intermediate-advanced bubble science posters and graduation finale poster.

2. Cut out a piece of butcher paper twice the length of narrator. Fold in half and cut hole in center for head to slip through. Add posters to front for each scene. For a bubbly effect blow up some balloons!

Narrators

1. Write script to include introductory bubble facts and explanation of bubble science projects. Practice using a loud and clear voice!

Camera Crew

1. Learn how to use a video camera.

2. Practice using the camera.

3. Begin filming.

Characters

ALL students

How To Become an "Official Bubbleologist" *(cont.)*

* Keep rolling 'em! Next, film the narrator with the beginning bubble science poster while reading the written script. Then, film students actively performing the beginner level bubble projects. Narrator should give objective of the project and procedures and show the results! Film a student reading a bubble poem or story or show some bubble science projects. Next, film the graduation poster. End the film with a big bubble bang, have all the students blowing bubbles with different types of bubble wands! After showing the film, hand out the bubble diplomas!

Bubbleologist Graduation Hats and Diplomas:

1. Have students work in pairs; each will need an 8" x 10" (20 x 25cm) piece of white construction paper and a 2" (5cm) wide colored band measured to fit their heads.

2. Students decorate one side of white construction paper with bubble design. Use crayons, markers, glitter, colored pencils, or paints.

3. Make a tassel by cutting a 10" (25cm) piece of colored yarn. Make stencils out of the ornaments on this page for students to trace and decorate. When complete, add to end of the tassels.

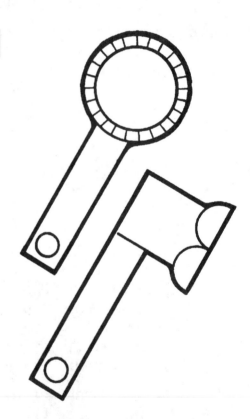

4. Assemble hat by first stapling colored band to desired size. Place decorated side of white paper face down. Center the colored band on it. Tape inside edge of the band to plain side of the construction paper. Glue end of yarn to center of white construction paper with bubble ornaments draping over side of hat.

5. Copy bubbleologist diploma on page 78 for each student.

Yummy Gummy Ice Cream!

Use your favorite store-bought or homemade vanilla ice cream recipe. Then sprinkle some tiny pieces of bubblegum on top of the ice cream. Enjoy!

Bulletin Board

Objectives

This interactive bulletin board has been designed to introduce and review bubble facts. It can also be adapted to use as reinforcement or enrichment in science, math, reading or language arts.

Materials

Butcher paper; colored construction paper; tagboard; white or blue cellophane; tissue paper; pushpins; hole punch; stapler; scissors.

Construction

1. Reproduce patterns (pages 72-75) onto appropriate construction paper. Cut out.

2. Cut bubbles of various sizes from cellophane.

3. Cover bulletin board with butcher paper. Use tissue paper to make grass. Add a title and assemble pieces onto bulletin board background; attach with staples or pushpins. (See diagram above.)

4. Write bubble questions on the large bubbles (see pages 56, 60, and below for ideas). Hang on bulletin board with pushpins. Punch holes at the top of small bubbles; write answers to the bubble questions on them and store in bubble jar. Use as directed below.

Directions

As an introduction to the bubble unit gather students around bulletin board display. Discuss bubble questions inside large bubbles (What is a soap film? What are bubble colors? Why do bubbles burst? What is bubbleology?). Find correct answers in the bubble jar and hang on large bubbles' pushpins. Return answers to bubble jar. Allow students to practice during free time.

Extension: Use to practice other skills. For example, to review syllabication, label bubble cards with spelling or sight vocabulary words. Label large bubbles "one syllable," "two syllables," and "three syllables." Write answers on the back of bubble cards. Students match word on bubble card to the correct large program bubble. When all bubble cards have been used, students turn over the cards to self-correct.

Bulletin Board Patterns

Bulletin Board Patterns *(cont.)*

Bulletin Board Patterns *(cont.)*

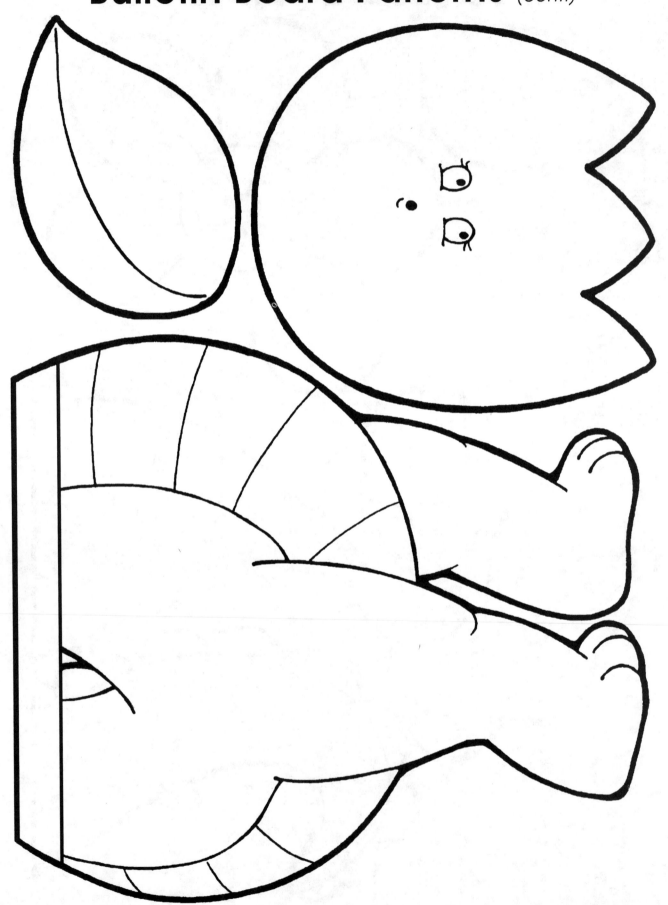

74

Bulletin Board
Patterns *(cont.)*

Bubble Stationery

Bubblegrams

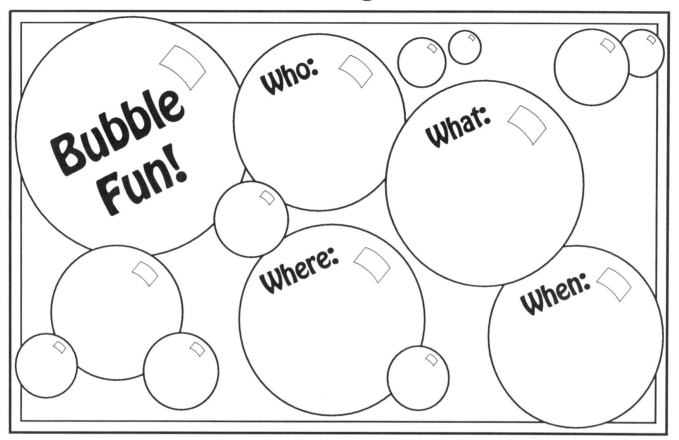

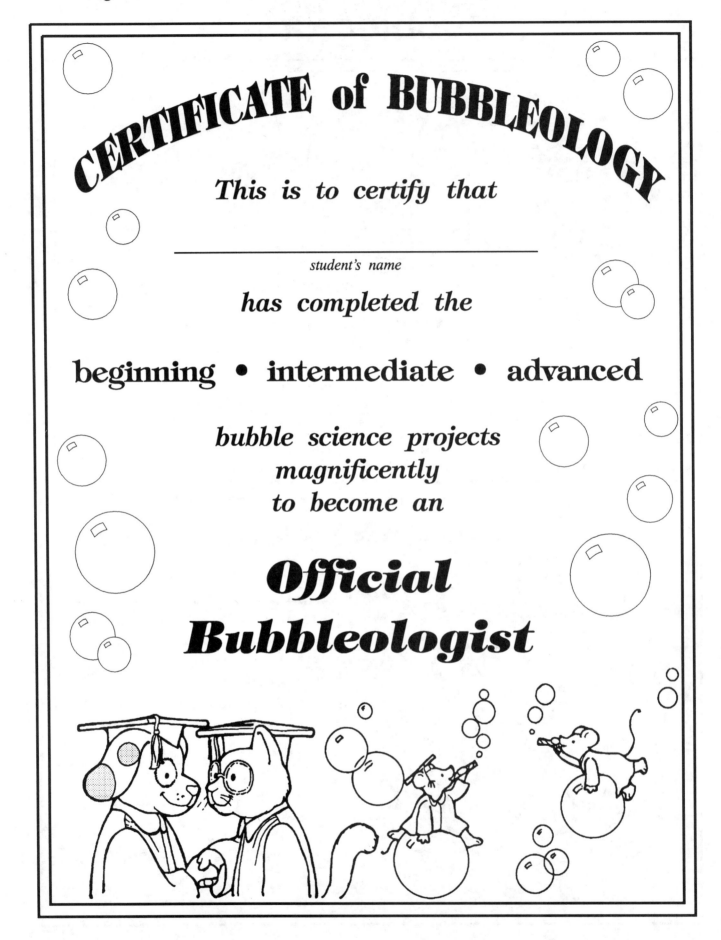

CERTIFICATE of BUBBLEOLOGY

This is to certify that

_____

student's name

has completed the

beginning • intermediate • advanced

bubble science projects
magnificently
to become an

Official
Bubbleologist

Answer Key

Story Frame   p. 13

1. baby-mother-father frog
2. Baby frog keeps swallowing bubbles
3. He floats away

Bubble Journey   p. 14

lived, bubble, air, made, little, soap, hit, rainbow, started, POPPED.

1. air
2. light is reflected
3. It's going to POP!

Deep Dive   p. 46

Examples: nap, cap,flap,lap,gap,map,rap,sap,tap,zap

Jumble Sentences   p. 47

1. Joe is chewing bubblegum.
2. What time is it?
3. Clowns are funny people.
4. Put the book here!

Who, What, When, Where of Bubbles   p. 48

Who: bubbleologist, bubble blower

When: daytime, after a rain

Where: on the tabletop, in a jar, outdoors

What: rainbow colors, soap film, bubble wand

Clothespin Story   p. 49

1. Marybeth
2. tubular
3. window
4. red petunia leaves
5. every morning
6. counts to 15
7. bubble fly

Frog Race   p. 53

1. #3, 2
2. answers will vary

Bonus: tadpole

Bubble Count   p. 54

1 a. Jen
   b. Kino
   c. 15
   d. 8
   e. 4
2 a. 9
   b. Jen - 2
       Kino - 5
       Bub - 4

Bubble Colors   p. 55

First row: 6, 12, 16, 14, 10

Second row: 10, 8, 7, 8, 6

Third row: 12, 8, 12, 8, 15

Bubble Game   p. 60

1. air
2. red, blue, green, purple, yellow, white, black
3. round-circular
4. air currents
5. No...depends on size of bubble wand
6. Bubbly hands
7. varied answers
8. varied answers
9. POP
10. varied answers
11. yes, water drops at bottom of a bubble
12. varied answers
13. after a rain
14. domes-geometric shapes
15. bubbleologist
16. varied answers
17. 2
18. varied answers

Bibliography

Fiction

Mayer, Mercer. *Bubble! Bubble!* Macmillan, 1980

Daver, Rosamond. *Bullfrog and Gertrude Go Camping.* Dell, 1980

Schubert, Ingrid and Dieter. *The Magic Bubble Trip.* Kane Miller 1985

Vesey, A. *The Princess and the Frog.* Little, 1985

Winer, Yvonne and Carol Aitken McLean-Carr. *Never Snap at a Bubble.* Educational Insights, 19560 S. Rancho Way, Dominguez Hills, CA 90220 (phone: 213-637-2131), 1987

Nonfiction

Baggart, James. "Bubble-ology". *Science World Magazine.* Sept. 8, 1986, pages 22-24

Cassidy, John. *The Unbelievable Bubble Book.* Klutz Press, 1987

Faverty, Richard. *Professor Bubble's Official Bubble Handbook.* Greenleaf Ventures P.O. Box 217, Schenevus, NY 12155 (phone: 607-638-5435), 1987

Florian, Douglas. *Discovering Frogs.* Macmillan, 1986

Mayfield, Margie. *Bubbles and Brainwork.* Science/The Children, 1979, pages 7-8

Oz, Charles. *How Does Soda Get into the Bottles?* Simon and Schuster, 1988

Petty, Kate. *Frogs and Toads.* Watts, 1986

Schechter, Bruce. "Bubbles That Bend the Mind." *Science,* March 1984, pages 44-50

Zubrowski, Bernie. "Memoirs of a Bubble Blower." *Tech. Review,* Nov-Dec, 1982

Zubrowski, Bernie. *Bubbles.* Little, Brown, 1979

The Exploratorium Magazine: Bubbles (1982) Copies available from: The Exploratorium, 3601 Lyon Street, San Francisco, CA 94123 (phone: 415-563-7337)

Poetry

Hillert, Margaret. "Blowing Bubbles" *Read-Aloud Rhymes for the Very Young. Knopf,* 1986

Payne, Nina. "Bubble Gum" *The Random House Book of Poetry for Children.* Random House, 1983

Teacher-Resource

Barber, Jacqueline. *Bubble-Ology.* LHS-GEMS, University of California, Berkeley, CA 94720, 1986